# SOCIETY UNMASKED

## Voices of Teachers and Students in Unprecedented Times

Edited By Kimberly Lewinski, Trent McLaurin and Bob Vogel

*Society Unmasked: Voices of Teachers and Students in Unprecedented Times*

writersmatter.org

Editors: Kimberly Lewinsky, Trent McLaurin and Bob Vogel

Contributors: Jaida, Joshua, Lisbeth, Charlotte, Aniya, Jung, Indri, Cymthia, Genesis, Brianna, Amarah, Aaron, Sloan, Anabell, Gina Martegus, Elliott, Eleanor, Lilian, Mariyah, Chloe, Christine, Amilly, Tate Diamond, Josiah, Jihad, Paige, Adeline, Haziq, Marialis, Abdulakhir

Teacher Winners: Lori Odem, Tracey Orem, Paul Dominguez, Joan Carter Williams, Aubrey Stewart, Carl Jackson, Laura Seeley

Special Project Coordinator and Copy Editor: Joseph Samuel Rogers

Book Design: Joshua Ash

Consultant: Klare Scarborough

This book has been published with support from the PTS Foundation, the Berstein Family Foundation and the Kessler Foundation.

All royalties from the sale of this book will support Writers Matter educational programs.

*Society Unmasked: Voices of Teachers and Students in Unprecedented Times*

Cover image: *Carried Away* by Charlotte Yoeun.

This book is dedicated to the students and their teachers who have participated in Writers Matter over the years and especially to those students whose work appears in this publication. May the power of writing "empower" their voices for all to listen and understand.

# Acknowledgments

*Writing about my life this year opened my eyes to who I am and what I can be. I learned that everybody has bad times in their lives and no one is alone. Sharing and listening to others gave me strength, especially during this pandemic year. This year has taught me to be strong and to follow my dreams, never give up and take responsibility. I have learned not to be afraid and that I can succeed. I have learned what resilience means.........*

7th grade Writers Matter student

This book is a reflective journey of selected students and teachers as they faced the many challenges of a pandemic, political upheaval and the injustices of racism.

This book would not have been possible without the contributions of many of our Writers Matter students and teachers. Their honestly, insights and most importantly, their voices provided us with real life stories and experiences that provide us with a unique perspective of a year filled with personal and family challenges, loss of family members and the witnessing of racial tensions and political unrest.

## So, a special shout-out to our Writers Matter students and teachers

This book is dedicated to the thousands of students from Philadelphia participating in Writers Matter and to our Writers Matter teachers who persevered this year in a most challenging learning environment to empower their students to write.

We are also extremely grateful to the many principals from the School District of Philadelphia for their steadfast support of Writers Matter and their teachers.

Special thanks to our participating Writers Matter schools:

Charles W. Henry School
Edwin M. Stanton School
Feltonville Arts & Sciences
Fitler Academics Plus
General Louis Wagner Middle School
J. Hampton Moore School
Monsignor Bonner & Archbishop Prendergast Catholic HS
Penrose Elementary School
S.W. Mitchell School

We are grateful for the generous support of our major funders: PTS Foundation, Berstein Family Foundation and the Kessler Foundation.

A special thank-you to Joseph Samuel Rogers who served as our copy editor for this book and Special Projects Coordinator for Writers Matter.

Bob Vogel
Founding Director, Writers Matter

# INTRODUCTION

The COVID-19 pandemic catapulted a time of unimaginable change and disruption. Despite the shift that started for many on March 13, 2020 and continued through the 2020-2021 academic school year, teachers continued to teach, and students continued to learn all while the world around them underwent dramatic and often daily shifts.

This book captures the voices of the teachers and students through their writing during the 2020-2021 school year. During this year, our country dealt with a worldwide pandemic, political unrest and a fight for racial equality. Documentation of these unprecedented times is critical. We sought to capture the voices of all who have lived through these 12+ months. In our view, almost no group has been impacted more by the events of 2020-2021 than the teachers who have been on the front line since the start, and their students whose lives dramatically changed overnight.

In this one year, we were introduced to a worldwide pandemic that changed every aspect of our lives. We could no longer go to school, play sports or go to art class. Even going outside to play with friends and neighbors was forbidden. We ran out of toilet paper and food was scarce in grocery stores. We were told to stay home, wear a mask and wash our hands until our skin felt like it wanted to fall off. We were learning about a virus that could make people very sick or die. Each day we heard the number of cases and the death toll constantly rising. We were scared.

As we were trying to cope with the pandemic, we learned the stories of Breonna Taylor, George Floyd, Ahmaud Arbery and others who were victims of police brutality. These stories sparked great sadness and rage in many people who no longer wanted to remain silent. The Black

Lives Matter Movement was at the forefront and protests took place around the country, even around the world. We witnessed these protests, we witnessed how the protestors were treated and we heard their voices. Additionally, we saw an increase in discrimination towards the Asian American and Pacific Islander community who were being blamed for the pandemic.

We also experienced a change of power unlike we've ever witnessed in our history. The president's refusal to concede the election caused great conflict throughout the country. The conflict culminated in an insurrection where many US citizens stormed the capitol resulting in the loss of lives and many injuries.

The pandemic is not over, and we are still fighting for fair and equitable treatment of all people. But we are still here, and we have a story to tell. We encouraged teachers to share their stories and create safe spaces with their students to discuss their experiences. We combined trauma informed pedagogy with literacy to encourage students and teachers to share their experiences in creative ways. They have lived lives no other children and teachers in history have lived, and we want the world to hear it!

# Writing in the Time of a Pandemic

Tracey Orem
ELA Academic Teacher Leader

Writing is expression, connection, power, and emotion. Teaching is connection, expression, power, and emotion. How can I teach you to write when I am not with you in person? How can I not teach you to write when we are not together? When we are alone and frightened and anxious and I can't hug you? When all I can give you is my love and encouragement and support across a screen, all I can give is a way to pour it all out onto the paper, into the computer a way to let out all that is bottled up to give it life in writing and share it. You are not alone; Your words have power your emotions are valid. You have power. You have a voice. I teach you to write so that you can reclaim your voice and your power and your connection when it seems all of that has been taken away. Writing is expression, connection, power, and emotion. Teaching is connection, expression, power, and emotion.

## Life in the Quarantine

**Christine, Grade 5**

To view this piece, visit the writing contest section of the
Writers Matter website, www.writersmatter.org.

# A Trip Inside My Head During a Pandemic

**Marialis, Grade 8**

March 2020- "Awesome, we have two weeks off of school. Ugh! I can't wait to sleep in tomorrow. Let me go tell mom and dad. I am so excited! Oh God, we are gonna' have so much work to do when we get back. It's fine though; I can catch up quickly. Let me go call my friends and tell them. This is gonna be great."

April 2020- "I can't believe I haven't been to school in over a month, but I'm not complaining! I do kinda' miss my friends though. It's fine; we'll be back by next month I'm sure. I have to fix my sleeping schedule just in case we go back sooner than expected. I wonder what everyone is up to right now."

May 2020- "I can't believe that someone could be so cruel. That poor man died in such a horrible way. He had a daughter and a family. They're uniform and badge is supposed to make me feel safe, but every time I see it I get so scared. And he's not the only one either. It's so heartbreaking to see so many people dying because of their skin at the hands of the people who are supposed to protect us. God help the Earth."

June 2020- "It's been so long since I've seen anyone. These masks are starting to get on my nerves. I wonder how my family is doing. I miss them so much. I wonder how everyone from school is doing. I hope Wella is safe. Wow! These protests are really heartbreaking. Why are they harming the protesters if they are being peaceful? This world is so sickening."

July 2020- "I finally get to see my family after so long. Karina's belly is getting so big! I'm so excited to meet the baby soon. I can't believe Joniel is about to turn 2. I love what Nie did with her hair. Everyone looks so different. I can't believe I have to wear a mask around them. I can't wait for things to go back to normal."

August 2020- "So I really have to go to school through a laptop this year? Being optimistic is so hard. This world is falling apart. People are getting killed on the street and protesters are getting harmed. This is so scary. I wonder what's gonna happen during this school year. Maybe we'll get to go back in the middle of the year."

September 2020- "Okay, I got this. School won't be that hard. This will all be over soon. I don't really like showing my face on the camera. What if they see something weird in the background? My back is starting to hurt from sitting up for so long. I can't wait to lie down after this. I'm so tired."

October 2020- "Wow, I'm turning 14 in a couple of weeks. Time flew by so quickly. School is starting to get a bit difficult. The work is not making any sense to me. I'll be fine. I just gotta' focus better. I hope I can catch up soon."

November 2020- "Oh God, please not my mom! She has to be okay. We've been so careful. We clean all our groceries and we always wear our masks and we always wash our clothes when we get back home. How did this happen? Please I need her. God, please protect her. She has to survive this. I can't do this without her. Please don't take her from me."

December 2020- "I can't believe I have to spend Christmas without my family. All my assignments are starting to pile up, and I don't have the energy to even look at them. I feel so overwhelmed. I haven't joined class in a while. The teachers are probably very disappointed. But I am so exhausted. I barely have the energy to get out of bed and take care of myself. At least mom is okay. Thank you God for protecting her. I thought I would lose her."

January 2021- "This is so frustrating. I don't understand anything these teachers are assigning. I wish they would stop yelling at me and telling me that they're disappointed in me. I'm trying my best, but this is so difficult. I haven't been hugged in so long. I just want some reassurance that everything will be okay. Everything is so loud. I feel like I'm drowning. When will I stop feeling this way?"

February 2021- "I need to get up. It's been days since I brushed my hair. I don't have energy to do anything. I wish everyone would stop yelling. I'm holding on by a thread. Why am I such a disappointment? I know everyone gave up on me and I don't blame them. I really wish someone would hug me."

March 2021- "Wipe your tears and get up. No one cares, and I have to deal with it. Everyone has something going on and I'm not the center of attention. I have such a hard time eating and sleeping. Why is my head getting so loud? I am so useless lately. I haven't been to class in a while. The one thing I was good at was School, and now look at me. Everyone expected better from me and I let them down. I wish I could find energy to care but I am so exhausted. I don't care about anything anymore. I just want someone to sit down and listen to me without telling me that I need to do better. I want my normal life back."

April 2021 (now)- "I can't believe I let myself get this bad.

I am trying to be myself again, but I just can't. Every time I think that I'll be okay, something reminds me of the person that I became. I'm probably gonna fail this year. There's no point in trying anymore. I give up. I just wish that I could escape my own thoughts. When will I be myself again?"

Chaos

By: Anabell, Grade 8

# Eternal Nightmare

Cynthia, Grade 8

We lost our summer.
Concerts at home
School at home
We lost our sunset
I'm left alone
On the evening
Of an endless March 13th
My days being wasted as soon as I wake up
Trapped in my cold room
No vaccine
The clock has lost the weather
We are stuck in the eternal nightmare
We lost our summer
We lost each other
Give us back our summer
The whole world seems so dark
Why must you hurt each other?
Your skin color and race does not define another
The screaming, the sorrows, the anger
When will it stop?
The flowers blooming brightly
I miss those days
Give us back ourselves
It's all gone

A day or two, a week, month, year
I'm walking alone in place
Going nowhere
A nightmarish week after another month, a year
I want to see our shining, shimmering summer once more
It's long gone
Hiding my sorrows behind a stifling mask

The summertime
The day we longed for
Please don't disappear
The opportunities we lost
The memories we lost
They all wander in our stolen summer
When will this eternal nightmare end?

# Suspended

Charlotte, Grade 8

Days pass.
They never last.
Here comes spring. Dangling on a string. The grass is green,
Yet we stare at a screen. May the sick get well, While I sit in
my cell. And hope we
can say "Coronavirus, farewell!"
Smiles are contagious
But so are the germs.
Remember to wash your hands until they're cracked and
firm.
6 feet apart---


While the rest are 6 feet under. Will the world get back
to normal? Every day, we wonder.
Protests rage
Negativity upstage.
But when will it be time
to turn the page?
Cut the strings And re-engage?

# PANDEMIC

# Writing in a Time of a Pandemic: My Story

Carl Jackson
3rd grade teacher

Wow! What a year! I remember the day our school had closed - Thursday March 12, 2020. I was warned that I should take anything of necessity because we wouldn't be coming back for a while. The kid in me came out very quickly: "No School!" It's the wanted snow day feel that we had not received because it was a mild winter. JACKPOT!!!!! It went from yeah this is really cool to hmmmmm this is really strange. We had a couple of weeks before spring break, so it was like an extended break. I, like most, cleaned closets, rooms, corners in the house. I worked out religiously. I met with 4 other teacher friends calling ourselves THE POD! I did my virtual Hot Chocolate Run which definitely felt strange because I didn't have that competitive edge I thrive on while running. Instead, it was an "oh well you accomplished your goal." Then after break we were told we would be returning virtually. Wait! What? How does that even work? I started to get nervous, but it was not as bad as I imagined. We were home safe and giving district made lessons. The days were still fun. I met with The POD almost every other week as we began with my 50th birthday. It was cute. They bought pizzas, balloons, cake, and adult beverages. This was awesome, but wait, was it? Many people kept saying I am so sorry we can't celebrate this milestone birth date. I got kinda confused because I was happy how it went. We social distanced and celebrated the way that I saw as fun. As time went on so did the UPRISE! UNJUST POLICE KILLINGS,

PEOPLE OF COLOR SLAIN, ANGRY, SAD, BOTHERED, WORRIED! We still were signing in and having lessons. Kids telling you how the feel which was like myself and others felt. Next came the work-place mentioning that a change needs to take place. BLM matter protests launch all over the world (It's time for a change (AGAIN)! This time things seemed more URGENT! We are seeing people speak out and speak up rather on my block, on internet, or even the View. Everyone wanted and needed to be HEARD! Unfortunately, some decided to use this moment of togetherness as a weapon. Looting and vandalizing became the forefront almost distracting us for the CHANGE we so desperately needed. THEN CAME CURFEWS! WHAT! Fear sets in I am scared to even go outside. I am a black man and now feel like a TARGET all over again. Will I be seen as a potential threat to law enforcement? Will I appear as threat to people walking near me because I could be considered a looter or an angry black man who wants revenge. YIKES! This is now starting to not be so fun. We can't see our family; we MUST keep our distance. I must wear a mask that just may scare folks because of the color of my skin. Meanwhile, I need to wear the mask to keep myself and others safe as daily reports show the growing cases and deaths because of Covid-19.

Fast Forward - Part 2!

Wow so much unrest has been endured and now it's back to school and teaching FULL days. The ANXIETY builds from ALL (Teachers/Parents/Children). But look at God! Won't HE/SHE DO IT! We are making it through COMMUNICATION, PATIENCE, PERSEVERANCE, and UNITY! We laugh at my technological mistakes and learn from them. Students and even some parents are teaching me as I teach them. We are writing using the "Reset Program" which has been a LIFESAVER! We are learning about each other through a screen versus in person and we ALL feel connected despite the obstacles and the hands we were dealt. It has not been easy but we (myself, students, parents) have been thriving. AGAIN, don't get me wrong it hasn't been easy. Carrying 35 more pounds, sitting all day with aches and pains as you get up to walk to the kitchen to get something else to eat/drink. Starting some days at 5am and not stopping until 6pm. Working weekends when you are determined only to give 23 hours that turn into 6 hours. Not seeing some of your close friends on "The Regular" can be rough. Some you lose touch with and others you Zoom more with can be a juggle. The no pacing yourself can be overwhelming and cause burn out. Some days are better than others and you must hold on and cherish the glimmer of hope/happiness that beams during various times during the day. Through it all I have seen my students SHINE and RISE to the occasion... You can see it in our morning meeting which begins with music and dancing as we come on led by yours truly. We have daily Temperature Checks/ Question of the day that we share in the chat and aloud (for those who want to share). We have energetic classes. The students were made aware from the very beginning that they have a VOICE and it needs to be HEARD! We have used the "Reset Program" and have learned so much about each other. We respect one another and know that we are ALL EQUAL and BEAUTIFUL CREATIONS as we respect our differences. WRITING IN A PANDEMIC HAS MADE A DIFFERENCE IN ALL OF OUR LIVES! As we continue to shift back into the physical (in-person) world of school we continue to sense excitement and fear. I have been vaccinated and see that the next wave is fast approaching. Maybe we are getting back to some normalcy or at least another step closer. I definitely feel like this summer will be a RESET for myself as I pray to be able to go away and RECHARGE. Hopefully you will be able to as well!

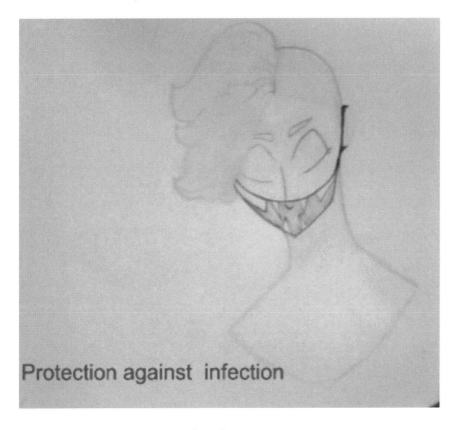

Protection Against Infection
Anabell, Grade 8

# Life in a pandemic: The world was on a pause by default

**Amarah, Grade 7**

P-eople struggling with the lock down process

A-ll, whether young are old, is subject to getting it

N-o one is safe from the virus

D-etermind to find a vaccine to fix the crisis

E-ducate the public with correct information

M-assive amounts of deaths rise in elevation

I-solated from everyone no school more desperation

C-onducting analysis and experiments of the situation so
we can live our lives once again

# Nothing But Hard

Jaida, Grade 9


Life in a pandemic is nothing but hard,
With quarantine, having to stay 6 feet apart, and postcards
Enclosed in a house that not everybody can call home
Virtual school having students using Zoom on Chrome
Everything ordered online, now there is always a package
at the door
The Black Lives Matter protest was only for justice and
peace because we need more
The police brutality and being called racial slurs
All these years without saying anything, this had to occur
But first we must use our voices until we succeed
Because justice and equality are all we need
An attack on the Capital once we got a new President,
Injuring some of the Capitals residents
The violence, the hatred it must be stopped
Away from the madness, holidays went and flopped,
No family on Christmas or Thanksgiving
Life in a pandemic getting really unforgiving
The workers, the helpers, and medical department
We thank you for everything you put yourselves through
Because of you, hopefully soon one day we can leave our
apartments
Once this is over life will feel good and brand new
Life in a pandemic is beautiful and enjoyed
Sleeping in and binge-watching Netflix and Disney Plus
Games with your family, in which them you always
destroyed
I am thankful for everyone trying to help us,
But for now, with this pandemic we have to adjust

# Covid Dynamics

Jihad, Grade 3

Things always change
In life's domain
You gotta learn how to deal with some pain
Accept things
That you can't change

Got an old mind
With young age
Everybody together
On this stage
But it won't happen on this page

Back and forth
Like ping pong
Call me a dragon
So I drag on
Love for both sides
So please get along
This is my pain
Wrapped in a song

We are dealing with something new
That no one knew
To my family
I stay true
Even though
They're not in my view
Pop Pop
Nu Nu
I really miss you


Friends I haven't seen
In a few
But we are still a team
Like Uncle Drew
So don't let this pandemic
Stop you

# Through Her Eyes

Paul Dominguez
4th and 5th Grade English
as a Second Language Teacher

I've watched her grow for 18 years

Let her form her own opinions

Be kind and fair

Strong for herself and others

Surrounded in a place with different values

Divided like our country

Not allowed to peacefully walk out of school

To end gun violence

She didn't understand why guns were more important
than student's lives

I get a call telling me her and two hundred twenty five

Got a Saturday detention for doing the right thing and went
with pride

Then she sees African Americans killed by those who are
supposed to protect

Goes to protests to show her support

And sees others yelling and cursing at them

I fear for her safety but let her stand for what she believes
in

She shares her thoughts and tries to persuade others
to change

And quickly finds how vile social media can be

A boy who haraasses her telling her she should go back
to her country and eat tacos

Tells her he knows where she lives and her boyfriend can't
be there all the time

The police are called and they respond she has been trolled

And in court that could have been interpreted as he might
come to say hi

This has not deterred her

She remains strong and undeterred

I am proud of the woman she is becoming

And sad to see the world she has seen at such a young age

through her eyes

# Alice

**Indri, Grade 8**

Alice, a girl who everyone loved, has brown eyes, brown skin, curls that touch her waist. Like any other 7th grader out there, she is very lively and fun to be around. She loved attending her art classes, reading, and playing video games. But everything flipped. A new virus has taken over China... it will be okay...right? No wait, it's in India, Paris, it is here... I can't believe it's finally here. Alice had no choice but to stay at home and could no longer attend her art classes or school. March 14th was the day she attended remote class for the first time in her whole 12 years of living. A month later, a worldwide rule insisted on citizens wearing masks every time you go outside. She hated the feeling of wearing one. It felt like jail, but she knew she had to keep it on for the sake of her loved one's lives and others. It is all such a burden wanting to go outside, yet too scared to do so. She was getting used to the new regulations, but June really sucked the life out of her. She saw people who looked like her getting killed just because of their skin color and being treated unfairly and labeled as "dangerous." This made her angry, upset, and sick in her stomach. More and more reports on police brutality started to show in the news and social media up to the point where Alice is deathly afraid to be near a police officer; she shouldn't have to feel this way she was only a kid...only a kid. It kept on getting worse. January 6, 2021, angry Trump supporters crashing and storming the Capitol just because they couldn't get over Trump losing...what a shame but she was glad Biden took over. She has high hopes for him to make this whole tragedy to be over. Everything went black. She can no longer touch nor hold. EVERYTHING STOPPED! She looked over at the only visible thing she could and saw it was a mirror. She is translucent...a moment of realization sets in. She had been dead a week after the storm of the Capital. She had gotten infected by Covid-19 she had been watching a recap of her life all this time. Her family was telling the memories they shared with her all of this time....no no no how did this happened? Her surroundings suddenly changed; she now saw a scene of her family members gathered around her grave. Engraved on the head stone it stated "In loving memory of Alice Scar; killed by Covid-19 January 13, 2007-2021." She was glad she couldn't feel a thing while dying and glad her family is still there for her, even when she is gone.

# Tick-tock

Joshua, Grade 8

The world changed in an instant without warning
Our old life as we know it vanished in a blink of an eye.
Fear of the unknown crept upon us
like a leopard waiting for its prey
Working hard so the outside world
wouldn't get in the way
While the leaves decay in the late fall
Not having a basketball season left me
Walking into a brick wall
But I still stood tall,
Knowing I have to change and adapt
In this pandemic we call
But in this tragic turn of events
A great opportunity is what I saw
To reflect on life and focus on the real things
That matter is what I came across
You can't freeze time like the winter frost.
So I kept moving forward at whatever the cost
while not having regret over the time
That was lost.

# There Used to Be a Little Girl

Jordyn , Grade 8

There used to be a little girl
Smart, funny, and kind
She did well in school
She had loads of friends
Everyone loved her
But she began to spiral
Falling into a pit of despair
Burning the light out until there was nothing left
Trying so hard to please
Where did that little girl go?
She feels like getting up is a chore
It takes too much effort to start the day
Just to sit at her computer
As the world goes around her
As she stares numbly at her screen
For hours on end
Then she goes to sleep
Ready to do it all again
When will this end?
The days begin to consume her
The same routine
The same people
The same life
She has to tell herself
You'll be ok
But what if I just continue drowning
Drowning in everything
Never telling anyone what's going on...How I feel
At the end of the day she lays in bed...Falling asleep
Wishing to never wake up
Because it hurts more to wake up.

# THIS IS SERIOUS

**Aaron, Grade 6**

You monster!
You took people's dreams and careers.

Every time I see you
I get the shivers on my back.
Cries and breaking hearts.
You have no regrets.
You're a killer and murderer;
Have taken people's souls and lives.
You destroy relationships and families.
I am grateful that your power is not taking me away.
Your power is weak and you will never take me
because all people together we can defeat.
Soon you will be gone.
Millions of people have suffered
by their loved ones being gone
from this beautiful earth.
But in this world
people need to wear a mask to stay protected
from this monster.
But people don't listen because they don't
wear their masks
and you know what happens,
they get the COVID-19.
This quarantine has changed people's lives
from good to bad or good to crazy.
We people know that quarantine is not good
but there is no other way.

So I hope this poem helps you to know
that this is serious
and don't take this as a joke.
I hope you're ok
and have good health.

# The Little Things

Sloan, Grade 7

It's the little things in life that bring us together and give us joy.
Like when you meet someone new at a workshop or on the
street and find out that you both love the same band.
Or have the same shoes.

But now that we must separate to stay healthy, those joys and
interactions are gone.

So instead, we find different ways to connect and find comfort
in those simple little joys.

I, for example, have found and hung to these small things that
join us together with all of my might to keep from falling into
the vast, wide void known as isolation.

Like every Saturday evening, a few of my friends and I
virtually watch a movie together.
And how my sleep away camp has done virtual campfires so
campers can connect throughout the pandemic.

But as people are beginning to regain the little things that
bring joy to our soles, we are also losing other things.

Like being able to freely stand side by side.
Or kiss slowly.

These are things that, for some people, can't be cured by the
little joys in life.
For some people, not being able to go to work and school or not
being able to cough into your elbow without a face covering
on can never be able to be replaced by connections and virtual
calls.

I can relate in my own ways.

I can relate in not being able to see my friends
each day at school.


I can relate in being sick of virtual calls.
I can relate in being hungry for the touch of another person's
skin against mine.
To walk down the street next to my friends, arms brushing
each other as they swing side by side.


To being tired of my family.

But in the darkness, there always is a light.

I feel as if I know more about these people I call my family.
I feel that I know more about my friends' lives
and who they are.
I feel that all around me, my neighbors are growing closer.
I am growing closer to them as well.

So, what if my community may have been changed
due to this pandemic?
So, what if I can't turn this project in at school using my
bare hands?
In the end, it's the simple little pleasures in life
that keep us going.
Like that song that comes on the radio that you love.
Or the funny story your friend sends to you.


So, I told you how my community has changed.
How it has flipped into something that could be from
a sci-fi movie.
And how I use the little things in life that keep me calm
and sane.

Like writing this poem.
Or looking at pictures of my friends.


Or even the soft, cool moonlight that blankets me each night.
And if there is one thing I wish for you to think about after
reading this, it is how you are kept sane in these tough times.
It could be anything.
You could take up a different hobby.
You could start to redecorate your bedroom.


Or you could be like me.
You could focus on the little things and cherish them.
It doesn't matter.
But just remember that the little things are the sweetest in life.


And they always will be.

# A Pandemic Makes Me Feel Mad

Martegus, Grade 4

A pandemic makes me feel **mad.**

I can't go to school.

I can't be with **my** friends.

We have to wear m**a**sks when we go outside.

It's har**d** to breathe with a mask on.

I miss going on vacation to the beach.

It's hard to go places because everywhere is shut down.

The markets do not have a lot of food so we eat what we have.

I don't like staying inside.

I want to go to different place**s**.

They don't **a**llow too many people inside the stores.

Living in a pan**d**emic is extremely scary.

A pandemic makes me feel **sad**.

# Invisibility Mask

Elliott, Grade 3

We have to wear masks all the time. They feel really silly
even though I know they are helping stop the spread of the
Coronavirus. The mask on my face hides my true identity. It hides my smile. If I am smiling, no one can tell. I feel
like there is no point in smiling for pictures anymore- (although I still do). I sometimes wonder if people can tell my
true identity when I am wearing a mask. A couple months
ago, I wrote a poem about no one knowing my true identity
and it feels a lot like what is happening with masks. Here is
my poem.
It seems like people don't care how I am on the inside
People know me as beautiful, but it's just my outer beauty
they see They think they can know me by my name
They think they can tell everything that has happened by
my face They think they know who I am by my voice
I am more than what they see on the outside
I am a loving person, but they don't see my heart
I am funny, but all they see is me being smart
I am creative, but they only see me thinking inside the box
I am curious, but does anyone answer to my asking why
I care about others, but does anyone want my help
I am responsible, but do you trust me
I am bold, but you see me as scared
I am a leader, but do you think I would just lead you into
trouble
I am talented, but do you only see me when I fail
This poem feels a little bit like masks feel to me because
the mask hides my face and my face is where I show my
emotions the most. No one knows who I truly am while
I am wearing a mask. Masks make who you really are

invisible to others. Sometimes it feels like it is more of a mask covering who I truly am than a mask that is helping stop the spread of covid. It is like an "invisibility cloak" for your personality. And who wants to be hidden like that?

# In Morning Light

**Mariyah, Grade 5**

In morning light, I see gloom.
When the sun is bright, Flowers Bloom.
A Miracle Happens, A Poem Arises.
Stanzas in all different shapes and sizes.
All alone, cooped up in a box.
Everyone used to be a happy flock.
We now stay home, maybe forever.
Now even Animals have become clever.
A wave of Excitement used to be around,
Now it feels like a Ghost town.
We became like light, bright as a star.
We can be seen from a mile from afar.
We might feel small, sad and alone.
But at least we have a loving home.
We have a home and a family,
And the Morning ended Gracefully.

# The Pandemic

Amilly, Grade 5

Since the day 2020 started,
I thought it would be the best year of my life
But I was wrong
Instead it was one of the worst year of my life
Because I realized we were going to be in a pandemic
I had all these thoughts going through my head
"Is a pandemic even that bad?"
"Is the world going to end?"
I never thought a virus could spread so fast
To person to person,
To city to city,
To country to country,
It was like a giant wildfire that wouldn't go out
And the pandemic cases kept going up and up and up
It wouldn't stop
Many people were scared for their lives and others
Some people even looted stores for food since everyone had
to go on lockdown

# Dear 2045

Tate, Grade 4

Dear 2045,

Hello! I know we can't see each other for a while but I wanted to check in. Things are pretty crazy on my end. I mean, there is a global pandemic so we have to wear masks everywhere. Do you know what a quarantine is? I haven't even gotten into Black Lives Matter or Asian hate...Not to overwhelm you but Kobe Bryant died in a helicopter crash with his daughter Gianna and the California wildfires are getting out of hand.

People are cooped up in their houses. Everything is online and school is so hard. Families are going insane. Schools are opening up again and we are all stressed out. Meanwhile, more animals are continuing to become endangered and on the verge of extinction.

There is hope though! Vaccines are being distributed throughout the state. Good people continue to stand up and say enough is enough to Black people being killed by people who swear to protect and serve. Others are joining together to end racist attacks against Asian and Pacific Islanders. And we have our first woman VP in the White House. #seeherbeher. Oh... and there have been some good songs released to. I really like Billie Eilish as a new artist.

I would keep writing but my next class is in about 10 minutes, I gotta set-up Zoom. Google that if you don't know what Zoom is. Wait! Do you still have Google? Hope you're having a better year. See you soon.

Love, 2020-2021.

P.S. Let's catch up in a few years and maybe I'll have a dierent perspective.

Distant

Anabell, Grade 8

# Positive Through the Pandemic

**Paige, Grade 5**

The Covid-19 pandemic has impacted the way we learn, live, think and even breathe. When we walk outside it is like a wasteland. The grass is high and the ground is clean. No footprints, just masks. When we get to the store the carts are full to the brim. There are no canned goods, no toilet paper and no water. They're telling us to wear masks but where can we find them in stores. They're telling us to wash our hands, but we cannot find soap either.

Fast Forward to now, one year later. The pandemic is still sweeping the nation. Lots of kids are learning virtually and some are having a hard time staying focused. Many people don't have a place to work and lots of people have lost loved ones due to the virus.

With all the new challenges and changes, I have found a way to live my new normal. The biggest thing to staying successful in school has been my parents' support. I have a positive workspace and all of my supplies for class each day. All of my favorite snacks are nearby. I get up on time and get washed and dressed for the day, just like I was leaving the house for school.

My teacher has helped me a lot also. She is encouraging and has offered us a lot of extracurricular programs. To some people it may seem like more work, but for me it has kept my days full and let me meet lots of new people. I joined a Biodiversity program, which was 5 days a week of after school work and I even won the $175 Institute Award.

I was in a music program called #phillybeats, and also an art program where I learned digital art techniques in Procreate. I've stayed super busy and was able to keep my straight A's.

My family has always been super active, traveling the city and finding cool new experiences. This has also been challenging since the pandemic began. Luckily, once things started reopening, we have found some places we could enjoy while still feeling safe. We were at the Constitution Center on its reopening day, July 30th. They had timed entry, social distancing markers and they sanitized the seating areas after every show.

We have also been to the aquarium and the zoo. They both require reservations and are at limited capacity. We always make sure we feel comfortable wherever we are, and if it does not feel safe, we leave. We've even visited Disney World twice since they reopened and found that it felt really safe. I felt like we were in a bubble!

The pandemic has changed a lot, but it doesn't all have to be negative. I've spent more time with the people I love. I've made my living space more comfortable for my daily activities. I've learned to be very health and safety conscious. It's all about your attitude and what you do in the situation.

Positive Thru the Pandemic

Paige, Grade 5

# Dark Empty Halls

Genesis, Grade 6

Dark empty halls
Deep water fills it up, swimming in a virus
Hurting people as they fall in its path
This may not end or maybe it will just die down
The truth is that we lose more without much reason.
Our faces are covered for so much time
Outdoors
No longer a place to go, yet we still have people hurting
inside.
People in a doctor's office finding out the horrible news
While people don't have jobs
Ladies and men refusing to wear a mask, making more risk.
But one day this will change.
People who miss living their life may be granted a wish
To be happy and safe again...
One day we can live happy lives.
But that's a lot to say
We will try
Try as hard as we can
This world is not over yet.

Departed

Anabell, Grade 8

# THE YEAR OF NUMBERS

**Mrs. Lori Odum**
**6th Grade Literacy Teacher**

January joy on the first of twenty-twenty,
She's eighty years old, her birthday one of many.
No one knows the day nor the hour,
God has the final say, God has the power.

One-week later fire on the fifth floor,
Carried down flights by her son whom she adored.
It wasn't her hour nor time to leave us,
So, the birthday plan was absolutely a must.
A day filled with family, old friends, food and fun,
Queen for the day, mom was the center of attention.
Cards, gifts, flowers and much more,
She thoroughly enjoyed the stories they shared from before.
This would be the last time we'd gather in her honor,
Until she succumbed to the virus like thousands of others.
Positive results found me and brother too,
During quarantine we planned the perfect homegoing just
for you.
Almost thirty days later we gathered again,
Only ten could come say good-bye to your earthly end.
Twenty-twenty the year of numbers I'll never forget
Most melancholy day of May is eight, the day you left.
The memories we'll hold onto until the end of our time,
Your smile, your laughter, your sarcasm and always being
kind.
So rest on, Mom, your job was well done
Like God, the Father, and His only Son.

# Hello Everyone

Asher, Grade 5

Hello everyone, I would like to welcome you to year 2 of our
3-week lockdown. Man, this is really long.
Why is this virus so strong?
So i am here with my song,
To tell you what in my life i feel is wrong,

Through, all this quarantine
I felt like half of it was staring at a screen even though I
enjoyed staying home,
I still feel like this Virus has been mean

So, I hop on my phone looking for something to watch but
what I watch is not even what YouTube recommends,
So then I get on discord, to talk to my friends
And then I play games and read until my day ends

I want to get out,
I want to go to a theatre,
I want to be about,
I want to be able to walk, more than a meter

And then I saw blacks being treated poorly,
I heard them living their life, miserably
I wanted to help them and so did others, I didn't want them
to live their life unfairly

I've been trapped inside my home for days
I've wanted to go outside but there still are no ways
I want to see my friends but I can't,
Because the lockdown ending has gotten too many delays

And now it has been a year
That's how long I have been here,
I don't want to be kept in my house by covid's spear, and I
can't fight it because I don't have the gear

Oh, when will I be outside?
Covid, I have survived your tide
What do you want from me, you've made me lost and now I
need a guide?

What do you want from me?
Covid, I've been what you wanted me to be I know what
you've done because I can see I'm begging to be outside, I'm
on my knee.

# Writing during a pandemic

Josiah, Grade 3

I have never been a great writer. I have struggled with writing since I learned how to write. The pandemic has affected me on so many levels. I have several learning differences. I learn material differently than my fellow classmates. I do not always speak up when I should. When I am in class and my fellow classmates are looking at me. I get very nervous when I am asked a question or my opinion in front of the class. My writing has improved a lot this year.

Writing has given me a voice that I never even knew existed. I do not feel nervous when I write. It is easier to gather my thoughts when I write. I am no longer afraid to express my feelings in front of my classmates when my teacher asks me a question. The pandemic has affected my family in so many ways. A lot of my family members lost their jobs. I also lost my grandmother to COVID-19. My entire family was so sad from her sudden passing. I spent a lot of time with my grandmother.

My grandmother was my primary caregiver because my mom and dad have crazy work schedules. My grandmother taught me so much. I really miss her a lot. Everything changed when she died. I work harder in school because I know she would want me to do well and make good grades. Writing during a pandemic has had some challenges but through it all I managed to improve a skill that I once struggled with.

# SOCIAL JUSTICE

Anti-Racism

Anabell, Grade 8

# Boomerang!

Joan Carter-Williams
Teacher Leader, Grade 4

*Certain memories from your past can boomerang at full speed hitting you right smack in your face. A full-blown collision of past and present stopping you in your tracks when you least expect it. There's nothing you can do. It debilitates you.*

One day, when I was 10 years old, I woke up so excited for the day to begin I could hardly sleep the night before. Today we were going to go swimming at La Salle University. I had heard the pool was HUGE! I was so used to spending my summers in the city only getting wet with a garden hose. Sometimes, the adults on the block would turn on the fire hydrant at the end of the street. But to actually go swimming in a real pool was a dream.

I got up, took a quick shower then put on my swimsuit. I was super early. The bus wasn't arriving for at least 2 hours but I didn't want to take any chances. Finally, it was time to walk to the corner where the bus was waiting. I ran with tremendous speed. I wanted a seat in the back above the wheel. When the bus hits a bump, you would go flying up out of your seat. Fun right?

The bus arrived on the campus. The sun was blazing and its rays stretched far and wide. We walked the campus until we got to the building that was part of the gym. The smell of chlorine permitted the air. We were let into the building and then to the pool area and my heart was pounding. The pool WAS huge!

We were told to line up around the edge of the pool and listen to the life guard's instructions. "No running!", "No horse play!", "No diving!", "Wait for the whistle then jump in", he said.

I tuned out after that. My excitement got the best of me. My ears were trained for the sound of the whistle then there it was loud and sharp. I jumped in. The water was cool. I heard the sound of kids laughing and splashing.

Suddenly I realized that my feet were not touching the bottom of the pool. I panicked! I tried to wave my arms but I sank under. I went deeper and deeper. I couldn't breathe.

I started flailing around like a fish out of water but I continued to sink to the bottom of the pool. I couldn't breathe. It was eerily silent.I couldn't breathe. I started slipping off into a beautiful dream filled with the most amazing colors bright and brilliant. I'm not sure what happened next but now I'm out of the pool laying on the cold tile floor. My eyes began to focus as if I were being fitted for a new pair of glasses. "Which one is better? 1 or 2"? I could see a crowd had gathered in a circle above me. I could hear them but their voices were muffled. My sisters were crying. So, I started crying too. I heard the lifeguard say good she's breathing on her own now.

Boomerang!

It's because of this near-death experience that I feel somewhat connected to George Floyd during his last hours on May 25th.

Let me explain.

**The silence of impending death.** Face down still in handcuffs. **The muffled voices** as life begins to slip away from the body. **The crowd.** The ones filming and the ones yelling "Stop! His nose is bleeding"! Muffled voices. **The disconnection between body and soul.** Lifelessness.

I can only hope, through my tear-streaked face, that he saw those **indescribably brilliant colors** as he looked into the face of God.

# The Fight Against Xenophobia

Jing, Grade 6

There has been a lot of hatred and racism in this country. However, when the pandemic began, we continued to fight for justice and equality. Discrimination towards the Black community didn't begin during the pandemic. Rather, it has been deeply rooted in our country's history. The Asian American community and Pacific Islanders have also suffered greatly from the white supremacy in this country. Even though there is hatred in this world, it has also brought us together.

Racism towards the Black community didn't just appear recently.

Discrimination against people of African descent has been established long ago in our country. The seed of oppression and prejudice was planted during the slave trade where slave traders sold African villagers in exchange for money and goods. Despite the efforts people made throughout different generations, we still have a long way to go until achieving racial equity. People from the Black community are still treated with prejudice in some states.

Hate crimes targeted towards Asians have risen since the beginning of the pandemic. However, discrimination towards the Asian community originated long before the pandemic. The bud of racism regarding the Asian community grew when our country passed the Chinese Exclusion Act in 1882. This was the first time an entire group of people was banned from entering the United States based on their ethnicity.

It was only after 61 years that the Chinese Exclusion Act

was revoked. People of Asian descent have endured the unfairness for over a century, but even now there is still discrimination with regards to the Asian community.

It is proven that in this world there is violence and resentment. Although this is true, there also exists such things called kindness and contentment. There is so much loathing in this world, except it has also brought each and every one of us together.

When the lives of innocent people are brutally killed and attacked because of prejudice and racism, we fight for justice and for our voices to be heard. During the Black Lives

Matter protests and the Protect Asian Lives protests people from all different kinds of backgrounds, ethnicities, religions, genders, and sexualities all participated in the protests to bring justice and equality. All the hate in this world will try to divide us, but we will forever stand together.

This has proven that there has always been xenophobia and oppression in this country. When the epidemic began, we only continued to use our voices to fight for justice and racial equity. The inequality and racism towards the Black and Asian community wasn't set in place only recently. Xenophobia stems from the beginning of our country's history of the Slave trade and the Chinese Exclusion Act. There will always be hate and hostility in this world and they will always try and diverge us, even so we will always stand together as one.

# I feel locked inside

**Lillian, Grade 5**

I feel locked inside because I can't be who I want to be anymore. This world has changed me as a person and I don't

know if for good or bad. So, until we change this virus, I will stay locked inside my room like so many others.

Masks are supposed to feel like protection, but they make me feel alone like no one else understands me since I am covered.

I hear about new deaths daily, people who could have had better, longer lives but were killed never to reach the other side of the year.

Police brutality is horrible. The people who were supposed to protect us are hurting us. Just because we are all unique, everyone says we should be proud of our differences and I encourage that, but it seems like some don't. I can feel the burning anger inside and I understand why others let it become free but I don't understand why they let themselves be heard through violence when what we are fighting for is peace. We can't fight fire with fire.

Artwork by Anabell, Grade 8

# Colors of demise

Briana, Grade 6

Why did you do it?
Why did you choose to do it?
Was it because you thought it was the right thing to do?
Or your hatred,
Despising,
Seeing someone as dark as never even touching a bright
light.
You were here just doing your job right?
But you put your knee to neck,
Like if he were a threat,
Deciding if it would be best to just put him to rest.
He screamed...
He yelled!
"I can't breathe, please someone, help."
People gathered around to see what was going on.
But the last thing we knew...
He was gone.
Why did you do it?

Why did you choose to do it?
People started to fight because they knew
This was right,
But then a flash came and all has gone bad,
people are rioting,
are not surviving,
While people like you are thriving.
Why did you do it?
Why did you choose to do it?
As weeks go by,
Protesting for Black Lives turned into...
Fire at night...
More and more black people died
Due to what you thought was right
But was that worth more than people's rights?
Why did you do it?
Why did you choose to do it?
Things have gotten better,
But they'll never be the same.
Discrimination still lies within the brain,
Along with the hatred,
Along with the pain.

# CHANGE!

**Aniyah, Grade 8**

I am confused and afraid.
Those who are supposed to protect us
are shooting us down.
Bang! Bang! Bang!
Another innocent life taken;
Just walking down the street,
Something so peaceful turned into a death sentence.
"NO JUSTICE, NO PEACE," they scream.
James kills Mike.
Gets 25 to life.
Officer John pulled the trigger,
Goes home to his wife
No Justice, No Peace.
To serve and protect you say
Then taking lives
Like in a video game
In memory of the innocent
Things needs to change
We can't trust someone
who SHOOTS US down.

Bang! Bang! Bang!
NO JUSTICE! NO PEACE!
What next? I fear...
Little sister and me
Strolling down the street...just shot down
Or held at gunpoint because our skin is brown
Things need to change
Now and not never
We keep SCREAMING!!
NO JUSTICE NO PEACE!
It's like a broken record.

# Silent

Chloe, Grade 5

With so many lives being taken every day, they tell me to
stay silent? When a man was killed with a knee at his neck,
they tell me to stay calm? Too many lives are being taken
Too many lives are gone
And with more on the way
You expect me to say
"It's fine"?
I'm surprised the graveyards aren't filled yet.
And I'm not one to make a bet,
But if we don't do something
More lives will be lost.

# BLM Protest

Diamond, Grade 5


The people protesting filled the streets.
The cops were unsure what to do but seconds later shields
up and smoke bombs were all over.
But to my surprise they still protested, holding their signs
higher
When police brutality happens, emotions are high and
people start snappin.
And all you could hear were "Boom"
"Glass shattering"
"Yelling and police sirens"

Days after that, you could see broken pieces of buildings
and stuff was stolen.
Bad things are happening when injustice gets violent and
causes a riot. And some people ask why all this happened.
How would you feel if people hated you because of your
skin and not your actions?
I hate that all this had to happen, that someone had to die
for someone to realize you can't just take people's lives?!
Black people had to die due to police brutality.
Hate crimes happen by the hands of uneducated
indifferences. I see that different races have experienced
hate.
I see this has brought together our races from this same
hate. Someday, one day, this will end.
So we wait.

# INSURRECTION

# Undone

**Lisbeth, Grade 8**

It was January 6, 2021.
Votes were being counted to check who had won.
An angry mob stood outside,
on that day five people died.
At first it seemed like a normal day,
peaceful protests had begun last May.
But then hate is never peaceful, you know,
in fact, it's like venom, potent but slow.
So just like that it started spreading,
and I'm not talking about what caused the pandemic.
This can't be controlled by staying apart,
because it's not physical,
it's a problem of the heart.
The two are very similar in more than one way,
both dangerous, deadly, and don't know how to play.
And those couple of words that caused a spark,
a raging fire, illuminating but dark.
People hiding under chairs...
Children crying, parents scared...
Is this the world in which we're forced to live,
where fear takes over more and more?
With broken families,
tough beginnings, sadness,

Guns and death galore.
Am I the one remotely bothered?
Is there something wrong with me?
Because in this world that seems so pleasant,
nothing ever comes for free.
You laugh, you cry, you live, you die.
honestly, it's nothing new,
if only thoughts are what control us, we'll die not just one
death, but two.

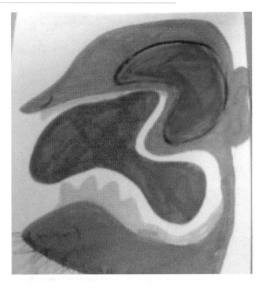

Corruption

Anabell, Grade 8

# What happened on January 6th

Eleanor, Grade 5

On January 6th thousands of Trump supporters stormed the Capitol building and injured 140 police officers. They broke through barriers and smashed windows. If they had taken the building, then our democracy would have been threatened. They did this because that's where the U.S. Congress was certifying the election results. And, all of this time, Donald J. Trump was egging them on.

What they did was illegal, because they have no right to go into the Capitol building. I think that many of these people don't want a democratic government; they want a Nazi-style government. This style has one dictator, who controls every aspect of citizens' lives, from what TV they watch to what stores they go to. If the Trump supporters had taken over, and Trump had a second term as president, then our country might have become a dictatorship. Terrorism is designed to make people afraid, which is mainly what the protesters were after. They wanted to scare officials into stopping the election.

It must have been incredibly scary to be in the Capitol building, feeling helpless and afraid. They had no weapons, and many of the protesters did. They didn't have a clear picture of what was going on. During the insurrection, I felt scared for my city. Philadelphia is an important city in our country's history. I felt that Philadelphia could have become a target for protesters. I didn't think that the protesters would succeed because from the footage released, I thought that their method didn't look very organized. I think that if they had been more organized, they might have taken the Capitol building.

I value our democracy because citizens get a say in the government, although it's not perfect when another political party wins. This hasn't happened in the history of our country, and I hope that it will never happen again.

Demise

Anabell, Grade 8

# REFLECTIONS

# Teaching in the Time of a Pandemic

Laura Seeley
8th Grade Literacy Teacher

In the spring of 2020, the reports of Covid came slowly at first, then faster and faster. Cases were in Italy and Washington State. Then New York City. Then near Philadelphia. Covid was declared a global pandemic and the School District closed down, at first for only two weeks. Two weeks became an indefinite period and students were given chrome books to talk home. School went online.

Everyone was uneasy and full of anxiety. Nobody knew how to protect themselves and their families against this unseen enemy. Hand sanitizer was sold out, along with disinfectant, bleach, and almost all cleaning products. The uncertainty of everything was so scary.

My last day in school was Friday the 13th of March, 2020. We only had about half of our students. We watched movies and waited for the day to end. I graded an assignment, the last one that we would complete in person. At the end of the day, I rode the elevator with two colleagues to the first floor, boarded the bus and went home. That was the last day that seemed somewhat normal in the spring of 2020.

When schools closed and went online, teachers posted assignments, held Zoom meetings and slowly adjusted to the virtual world. Certain students always attended class and we bonded through the screen and the frustrations. Many students disappeared, did no work and did not appear in class. Lost to the virtual world.

While school continued online and the pandemic swirled around us, people gathered on the streets for the Black Lives Matter protests. The incidents and videos unleashed a stream of anger that flowed into rivers of people. The anger was as thick as the heat that hung over the whole city. Windows were smashed and businesses looted. People marched again and again, trying to convert the anger and frustration into changes.

The morning of the biggest march, everyone gathered at the Art Museum, where there were speakers and music. The crowd was huge, a sea of people filling the parkway from the Art Museum to Logan Square and beyond. People everywhere. Wearing masks, shouting, holding signs. Supporting each other. There was a palpable feeling of change in the air. People felt it, they needed it, they cried for it.

As the school year ended, I missed graduation most of all. We had a virtual ceremony with awards, a guest speaker and everyone present. Parents, family, guardians and students. It just didn't feel real. Not a real gathering, not a real celebration, just one more virtual meeting to watch our screens. Virtual graduation was just not the same.

Without graduation marking the end of the year, time continued to slip by and move along, like water flowing. No markers of where it had been or where it would go. And so it would continue, time sliding through the year as spring flowed into summer and summer into fall. School started again and there were lots of virtual meetings. There was enthusiasm at first. Virtual school is new! Look at this online project I created! Eventually the newness wore off, the tarnish started to show and school became an ongoing problem of every day. Teachers were trying. Students were trying. Everyone was struggling.

Election Day 2020 became Election Week 2020, as votes were counted and recounted, the tensions mounted. Both sides cried fraud. Court cases were submitted and rejected as the vote counting continued. The election was called on Saturday morning and suddenly nothing seemed to matter. Work was unimportant, Covid was a distant thought and Philly was ready to celebrate. The whole city came out, shouting, honking and cheering from street corners. It felt like a release, like a win, like a new world.

Thanksgiving came and brought a feeling of normal in the abnormal year. Just having a familiar ritual was a blessing, even over Zoom, even from a safe distance. We shared food, talked and laughed together, holding on to as much normal as possible. Thanksgiving also brought travel. Covid cases and deaths were still high, yet thousands of people traveled for the holiday. Some wearing masks, some not. Many carrying Covid as a stowaway passenger.

Winter break brought Christmas and the New Year, marking time and bringing a feeling of the end and of a new beginning. Then came January 6th and the invasion of the Capitol in Washington DC. Time stopped. This was history. Bad history, dangerous history. A moment like no other where American citizens felt justified attacking the symbol of the American government. Shaky videos taken from camera phones captured the events, reflecting the confusion of the moment. Violence and chaos. Rumors flying. Someone had been shot, the crowd were protesters, they were rioters, they were insurrectionists.

We returned to school and slowly closed in on the anniversary of the shutdown, a year of virtual schooling. A year of staying home. A year of trying to recreate school in the virtual space. It was about this time, in January, that virtual school became really hard. Hours of Zoom classes with students. Hours of grading. Hours of creating assignments. It all became too much and there seemed to be no time for anything else. It was a dark time, a sad time.

Spring 2021 feels very surreal. Plants are growing, flowers are blooming, people are being vaccinated and hope seems to be floating in the air with the pollen. But, but, but. There is always a but. People want to get outside, see friends and return to some sort of normal, but there are still problems with Covid and infection rates are rising. We are nowhere near normal, yet we can almost feel it, almost see it, almost reach it. A year ago, in the middle of the uncertainty, with everything shutting down, I rode around Philly on a beautiful spring day. The uncertainty was rising, streets were mostly empty in contrast with the beautiful weather and feeling of spring. Perfect weather, perfect sunshine and a world that was falling apart. This year I did the same, riding around on a spring day, watching people. People are outside, wearing masks and enjoying the day. It is a different type of spring this year, a more hopeful spring, full of yearning for an end that we can almost see and full of hope for a future we can almost feel.

# Things will get better soon.

Adeline, Grade 4

Who would have thought? Just a *year ago* I was going about my business, asking my parents for play-dates, and eating in a restaurant every other day. But in a matter of weeks, it went from peachy and perfect to cramped up at home and having to endure a whole new lifestyle. For the first few months at bedtime when my parents were kissing me goodnight, my knees just shook violently. I couldn't stop them. And when I thought it had stopped-*twitch*. It took almost an hour to fall asleep every night. And what was worse, no one was prepared. No one was expecting for a pandemic to strike. No one expected for us to have to practically stay inside for this whole year of our life, and longer.

It's so hard to wear a mask everywhere. At first it felt like I had to suffocate anywhere outside I went. It felt unnaturally hot. It felt like I was powerless. Even now, when I'm awfully used to it, and if I imagine a year back, not wearing a mask sounds like it could never happen, I still have a little nagging feeling every time I put one on. But that's the world we live in. Since the vaccine came out, things have definitely improved, but it's not available to everyone. People who think they have nothing to worry about, could *still* very much be exposed! Then the organizations who give the vaccine to people think some of them have nothing to worry about, so they don't offer the vaccine to them. But then more reports roll in about those *same people* getting COVID.

But wait- there's more. The police decided to go and be horrible in an already horrible time. Police brutality is *very* upsetting. *Black Lives Matter*! Police targeted mostly people of color, which is devastating for the whole world of black people out there who had to go to bed with the thought that tomorrow they could die. And it was traumatizing for others too, they had to go to bed with the thought that people were going to bed with the thought they could die the next day. But one good thing- his name is Joe Robinette Biden. Now we could go to bed thinking about this: We have a president who is a kind man, is trying not to be racist, and can make good impactful decisions for our country!

Things will get better. Things will get better soon. Things *ought* to get better soon. You know, and I know- things will get better soon.

# Learning in the Time of a Pandemic

Abdulakhir, Grade 8

Through everything that's happened in 2020 with Covid, Black Lives Matter, the election, and the attack on the capitol, let's just say it's been crazy. Covid ended our lives practically. We were all stuck in the house without seeing the outside for days. Having to wear a mask every time we walk out the door or not being able to hang out with friends. Black Lives Matter started protest, riots, looting and even buildings getting burned down to be used as a voice. Black people were being killed because of their skin and then were not given justice. The election started questions, fears, and worries for our country's future and wellbeing. The attack on the capitol was a start of many questions, like why were they just let in or why weren't they attacked with force? Why weren't they attacked like the Black Lives Matter protesters? 2020 was an experience that changed not just my life, but billions of others.

In 2020 when covid first started, we were not really worried about it; we thought that after a while it would go away. Two months later, while I'm getting ready to go to bed so I can be up early for school tomorrow, my mom yells, "no school tomorrow". So, I jump up and go to her to see what she was talking about and she says, no school for the next two weeks. I instantly had the biggest smile on my face because no school for two weeks was like a paradise. But then two weeks turned into a month, and a month turned into 3 months, and 3 months turned into no school for the rest of the year. That "so called" paradise I had in mind became a prison that I couldn't leave. I couldn't see my friends anymore, I couldn't go places, and I was isolated from the world. A couple months later my mom had to leave her job to make sure that my siblings were doing their work. That's when I knew things were going to get bad, she kept telling me that we were going to be fine because she had money put aside, but that money wouldn't last us forever. After a while, I started to become used to being stuck in the house and not being able to see people. Truth be told, I had to become accustomed to it because this is modern life.

Then when the Black Lives Matter protests started. I didn't know how to feel, to be honest I was angry. I was angry because cops were getting away with killing innocent black people. But mostly I felt scared, because why should I have to fear the people who are supposed to protect us? The public tried their hardest to make the protesters seem like criminals and thieves, but truth be told they were not criminals. They were normal people who wanted justice for a long list of black people that were killed for no reason. When all of it started, I was actually at my cousin's house in North Carolina, and they were not protesting as much where I was, so I didn't get to protest. I tried my best to spread awareness on social media, but even then, there were multiple people who didn't agree with protesters and were against it. It soon became Black Lives Matter against All Lives Matter, but the only problem with that is the only life that really mattered in America was white people. So, they can scream all lives matter all day, but all lives can't matter until Black Lives Matter, Hispanic Lives Matter, Native American Lives Matter, Asian Lives Matter, and more.

Then last but not least the attack on the capitol started because Trump didn't win the election. When I first heard it happened, I was surprised but not really because they were already saying if Trump didn't win, they would do something. The only thing that surprised me is how they got in because there is NO WAY they broke into a highly secured place like the Capitol Building. There was very minimum force to keep them out of the Capitol. So, when the people noticed that, they said why weren't they using the same force on them like they used BLM protesters. Then that's when it all made sense — they were let in and they thought it would make Trump president again but it didn't. All it did was show the double standards of how white people can break into the Capitol Building and 99% of them come out uninjured, but black protesters who are protesting about their life are shot at, run over, pepper sprayed, beat, and more.

So, throughout 2020 it's been rough and it's pushed us to our limits, but in doing so we were stronger and were ready for what comes next. If anything, 2020 taught us how to prepare, it taught us how to prepare for the worst to happen no matter what. So even though we had a global pandemic, people protested for their life because they were being killed just for being black, people breaking into the Capitol Building. We didn't give up, we kept pushing and we are still pushing to see better days. So, 2020 changed the world mentally and physically, but we're still here.

WRITERS MATTER

# I Am From Where Writers Matter

Aubrey, Grade 8

**"I am from the cracks of the Earth, seen, but often overlooked..."**
  A teen amongst peers is rarely an open-book.
    Feelings of anxiety and fear flood their minds,
      Many feel secluded and wear a disguise.


**"I am from a prison of your words I always believe..."**
  Let's teach them the power in writing
    And make them feel free.
  Pick up a journal and put down the red pen,
    Begin to write about where you've been.


**"I am from where disaster struck and we are still standing strong.**
  **I am from where travelers go and feel like they belong."**
    Share the journey of your story,
      Create a safe space for students to shine in their glory.
    Commonalities are found & community is built.
      Identities woven together to create this beautiful quilt.

A world where kids drown in their sorrows,
    Avoiding the thoughts of tomorrow..."
Every writer matters in our classroom,
    Writing to unlock their potential to fully bloom.
Building confidence, day by day,
    Empowering students through writing, they can find
    their way.


"Screams from teens who just want to feel free,
    With their parents telling them who they should be."
        Students write the chapters using their voice,
            And through their story, who they become,
                is their choice.
Show your students you believe in them, and they will believe
in themeselves.
        Creations of art, novels, and poetry displayed on future
        shelves.


"I am from a place that made me tough,
    Years worth of wisdom in a month."
Endless amounts of life lessons, taught by 14 year old kids
Shaping who I am, showing me love, and forcing open my eyelids.
Write down your words of wisdom,
            Here, take my pen,
                use your voice to inspire the world again.

**Robert Vogel, Ed.D.**
Founder Director, Writers Matter
Professor *Emeritus,* La Salle University
vogel@lasalle.edu

I have recently retired from full-time teaching after 43 years at La Salle University and currently serve as Professor Emeritus of Education. I am the Founding Director of Writers Matter in Philadelphia and Israel and founding Co-Director of Leadership and Global Understanding at La Salle University. I earned my doctorate from Temple University in Educational Psychology and Organizational Development and taught three years for the School District of Philadelphia.

I have co-authored numerous articles and co-authored "Methods of Teaching: Applying Cognitive Science to Promote Student Learning (Feden & Vogel) - McGraw-Hill, 2006; Voices of Teens: Writers Matter (Vogel & Galbraith). National Middle School Association, 2008; Empowering Young Writers: The Writers Matter Approach (Yost, Vogel and Lewinski). Temple University Press, 2014; and Writers Matter: Empowering Voices of Israeli and Palestinian Teens -Cultural Narrative Building through Writing (Vogel & Adwan). 2016

**Kimberly Lewinski, Ph.D.**
Director, Writers Matter
Associate Professor, La Salle University
lewinski@lasalle.edu

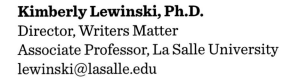

I am the Graduate Director and Associate Professor of Education at La Salle University and the Director of the Writers Matter Program. I earned my Ph.D. and M.Ed. from the University of Virginia in Curriculum and Instruction and Reading respectively. As a graduate student at UVA, I served on a Writing Across the Curriculum research team for three years and was an instructor of literacy courses at James Madison University. Prior to this, I taught for seven years at the elementary level. I earned my B.A. in Elementary Education from The Catholic University of America.

I have co-authored numerous articles and co-authored Empowering Young Writers: The Writers Matter Approach (Yost, Vogel and Lewinski). Temple University Press, 2014. Active in the literacy field, I am a member of many national and local literacy agencies including National Council of Teachers of English (NCTE), International Literacy Association (ILA), Association of Teacher Educators (ATE), Association of Literacy Educators and Researchers (ALER) and Keystone State Literacy Association (KSLA).

**Trent McLaurin, Ph.D.**
Consultant, Writers Matter
Assistant Professor, La Salle University
mclaurin@lasalle.edu

I have worked as a teacher, case manager, behavioral specialist, ABA therapist and director of special education. My practical experience, combined with my work as a researcher and professor, helped me blend the practical and theoretical gap that often eludes our schools, homes and communities.

My passion for providing strong supports for all students, especially marginalized youth, and ending the school-to-prison pipeline as motivating factors for my work.

I see the need for educators to be professionally trained by someone from outside their school community who understands education and mental health. My combinations of practical and theoretical experience as an educator and researcher drives my desire to provide support that is accessible for front-line educators, families and community providers.